# 101 WAYS TO HELP THE EARTH

## with Dr. Seuss's
# LORAX

With thanks to Tim Knight, Program
Director, Environment, Technology and
Economy, University of Maryland, for his
help in the preparation of this book.

TM & copyright © by Dr. Seuss Enterprises, L.P. 2021
Photographs used under license from Shutterstock.com.

All rights reserved. Published in the United States by Random House Children's Books,
a division of Penguin Random House LLC, New York. Featuring characters from *The
Lorax* ® & copyright © 1971, and copyright renewed 1999 by Dr. Seuss Enterprises, L.P.

Random House and the colophon are registered trademarks of
Penguin Random House LLC.

Visit us on the Web!
Seussville.com
rhcbooks.com

Educators and librarians, for a variety of teaching tools, visit us at
RHTeachersLibrarians.com

Library of Congress Cataloging-in-Publication Data is available upon request.
ISBN 978-0-593-30839-4 (trade) — ISBN 978-0-593-30840-0 (lib. bdg.)

Printed on 100% recycled paper

MANUFACTURED IN CHINA
10 9 8 7 6 5 4 3 2 1

# 101 WAYS TO HELP THE EARTH

## with Dr. Seuss's LORAX

by Miranda Paul

illustrated by Patrick Spaziante

RANDOM HOUSE 🏠 NEW YORK

# Contents

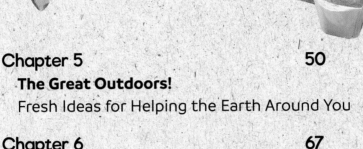

# A Message from the Lorax

Since the day I arrived
at this forest-green spot,
I've come to enjoy it.
I like it a lot!

Planet Earth is amazing
from ocean to shore.
Big mountains! Blue skies!
Awesome creatures galore!

But the Earth needs our help,
and I'd sure like to try
to clean up the land
and the water and sky.

Do you want to join me?
Being "green" can be fun!
I have some ideas
I will share, one by one!

# Introduction

Do YOU want to help the Lorax help the Earth? You *can*—and inside this book are 101 fun and easy ways to do so! Whether you live in the country or the city, these suggestions will help you make a difference. Most are free, and many can be done without help from a grown-up. And while some of the activities might *seem* like pure fun, they all offer a real chance to help the environment. It's true! You really can have fun while making the world a better place to live.

So what are you waiting for? It's time to start saving Planet Earth!

# IMPACT SYMBOLS

Each suggestion in this book helps the Earth in a different way. Some help reduce garbage or pollution. Others protect resources like water, wood, or fossil fuel. Others involve reusing materials or recycling them. And some directly help animals or plants. Look for these symbols throughout the book to understand how each suggestion helps the environment.

Reduces Energy

Reduces Waste

Reduces Pollution or Harmful Substances

Uses Less Resources

Conserves Water

Recycles/Reuses

Helps Animals

Plant-Friendly

# CHAPTER 1

# Earth Day, Every Day!

## Easy Things to Do Inside Your Home to Help the Planet

**#1** **TURN OFF YOUR NIGHT-LIGHT IN THE MORNING.**
Get into the habit of turning off lights. You'll save energy every day.

**#2** **BE A WATER SAVER.**
Don't run the water while you brush your teeth. Only turn on the water to rinse the brush or to fill a cup.

## #3 DRAW THE LINE! 💧

If you love taking a bath, try filling the tub only halfway to conserve water. Use chalk or bath crayons to draw a fill line halfway up the side. Or better yet, take a five-minute-or-less shower! (Bonus points if you turn off the water while washing your hair.)

**DID YOU KNOW?**
Taking a shower instead of a bath can save up to fifty gallons of water. That's shower power!

To **conserve** means not to waste, or to reduce what we use.

 **OPEN YOUR CURTAINS.**
(After getting dressed, of course!)
With the curtains open, you may not
need to turn on the lights to finish
getting ready.

# #5 WEAR ONE SET OF CLOTHES ALL DAY.

By wearing the same clothes all day (and not changing into new outfits), you'll make less laundry and save water. If you take off an item of clothing that isn't dirty, hang it up to wear again. Keep clean clothes out of the laundry pile!

REFUSE
REDUCE
REUSE

### REFUSE.
Avoid buying or using items made from—or packaged in—material that can't easily be recycled.

### REDUCE.
Choose goods that come in little or no packaging. Take care of things so they last a long time. Avoid waste.

## REUSE.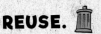

If something breaks or tears, learn how to fix it.
If an item is disposable or single-use, find a way
to repurpose it so it won't end up in the trash.

And last, but not least . . .

# RECYCLE!

Avoid throwing away items that can be recycled. Here's a basic guide to household items we can recycle.[1]

**YES**

tin and/or aluminum cans

glass bottles

paper and cardboard

rigid plastic containers and bottles

**Recycling** is a process in which machines break or melt down items so they can be made into new ones. Recycling helps to reduce pollution caused by our waste. Specifically, recycling keeps our landfills from filling up too quickly.

anything made of Styrofoam, including egg cartons, cups, or containers

anything with food scraps on it, like pizza boxes

broken glass or dishes

plastic wrap

1. Always check with your local facility for details, because each center runs differently.

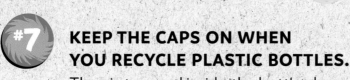

## #7 KEEP THE CAPS ON WHEN YOU RECYCLE PLASTIC BOTTLES.

The air trapped inside the bottles keeps them from getting flattened. Flat plastic bottles can accidentally slip into the machine that sorts out paper from other materials at recycling centers. When that happens, the plastic can ruin a load—which means a lot of recyclable paper ends up getting thrown away!

You may be surprised by some of the things you can reuse and recycle! Turn the page for even more ideas.

ECO-JOKE:

Instead of throwing away old amusement park rides, what should people do?

Whee-cycle them!

# #8 RECYCLE SPECIAL ITEMS, TOO. ♻

Items that *can* be recycled but need
to go to special drop-off centers include:

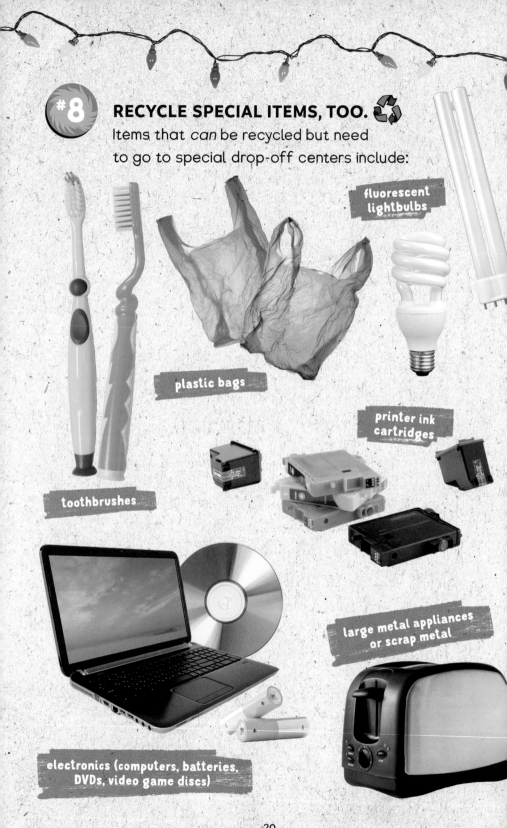

**fluorescent lightbulbs**

**plastic bags**

**printer ink cartridges**

**toothbrushes**

**large metal appliances or scrap metal**

**electronics (computers, batteries, DVDs, video game discs)**

holiday lights

crayon

crayon

crayons

crayon

eyeglasses

Ask a grown-up to search online for special recycling bin locations or mail-in donation instructions. Terracycle.com and Earth911.com, for example, are websites where you can type in a specific item to find out how to recycle it. Many grocery stores have recycling bins for plastic bags.

# #9 – #14 UPCYCLE! ♻

Upcycling is like recycling, only simpler. To upcycle something means to take a useless or old item and turn it into something new and useful. A grown-up can help you use a search engine to find instructions for all these crafts and more.

## 9. Toilet-Paper Roll Animals

## 10. Mismatched-Sock Puppets

## 11. Milk Jug Dollhouse

## 12. Plastic Bag Necklace

## 13. Tin Can Pencil Holder

## 14. Plastic Bag Jump Rope

## #15 MAKE A REUSABLE BAG. ♻

Turn an old T-shirt into a handy tote! You can use this kind of bag for light loads, such as a picnic lunch or when purchasing small items.

# STEPS:

**1.** Cut the sleeves off an old T-shirt.

**2.** Cut the collar off so the neck opening is wider and deeper.

**3.** Cut fringes along bottom of shirt about 1 inch apart.

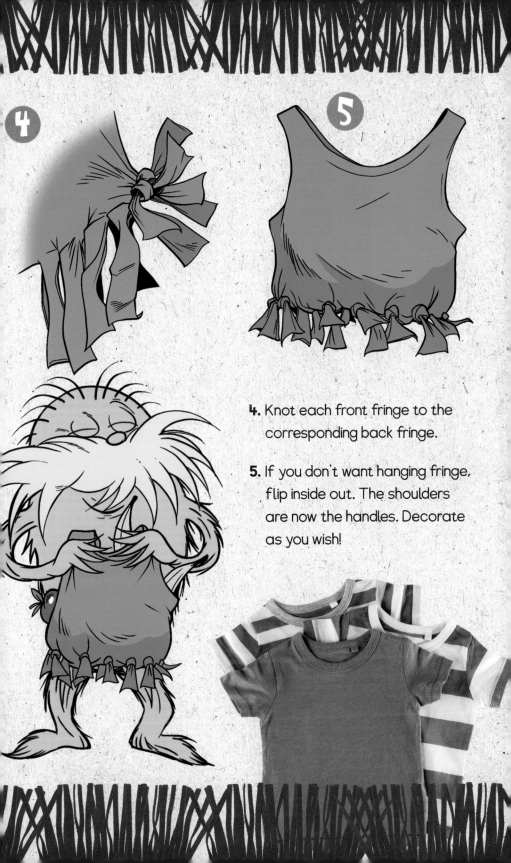

**4.** Knot each front fringe to the corresponding back fringe.

**5.** If you don't want hanging fringe, flip inside out. The shoulders are now the handles. Decorate as you wish!

# #16 MAKE STICKERS!

Want to help your family remember to help the Earth?
Ask your parents or caregivers if you can put stickers
on wall switches with reminders about turning off
the lights. Make the stickers by cutting squares of
masking or painter's tape and writing on them. Or you
can print or buy paper stickers instead.

# CHAPTER 2

# Green Your Plate!

## Food and Drink Ideas to Reduce Your Mealtime Impact

 **#17**

**CLAIM YOUR CUP!**
Choose a cup that's "yours" and use it
throughout the day instead of taking a new
one each time you're thirsty. You can label it with your
name so it doesn't get lost or used by someone else.
And when it's time to buy a new cup, consider
choosing a metal one—metal cups last a long
time and are eco-friendly.

# #18 FIND A SUSTAINABLE STRAW. 🗑

What other ideas can you think of to replace a plastic drinking straw?

licorice

silicone

bamboo

round wafer cookie

metal

paper

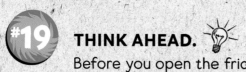

## #19 THINK AHEAD.

Before you open the fridge or freezer, picture in your mind what you want. The longer you keep the door open, the more energy it takes to cool the fridge afterward.

# #20 LISTEN TO YOUR STOMACH, NOT YOUR EYES! 🗑

Before you fill your plate, ask yourself—how hungry are you? Try not to take more food than you can eat. You'll use less of the Earth's resources and reduce waste.

**DID YOU KNOW?** 💚
Food we throw away can rot and spread harmful germs to hungry wild animals. When we take only what we can eat, we prevent food waste.

## GROW, DON'T THROW! 🌳
Got a potato or onion growing shoots?
Replant it instead of throwing it away.

**1.** With an adult's help, poke holes in the bottom of a tall, recyclable container.

**2.** Fill the container with potting soil.

**3.** Cut and bury the pieces with shoots. If you are separating onion shoots, be sure to keep them attached to their roots (you can remove the outer layers of the onion). For potatoes, cut one potato chunk per shoot. Make sure the chunks are about the size of an egg.

**4.** Keep your plant watered and well fed. Onions like bright sunlight, but potatoes can be put in a spot that gets some shade. Be patient!

# #22 – #27 KITCHEN UPCYCLING!

Food and drink packaging make up a large portion of the world's litter pollution—especially in the oceans. Finding ways to reuse and upcycle these items keeps them from entering landfills or making their way into the water. Here are some ideas to try!

## 22. Eggshell Flower Mosaic

## 23. Yogurt Container Photo Holder

## 24. Egg-Carton Boat

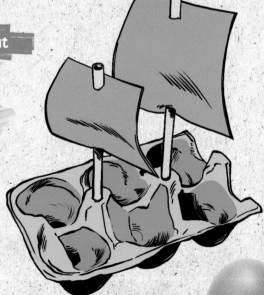

A grown-up can help you use a search engine to find instructions for all these crafts and more.

25. Plastic Bottle Bowling

26. Popsicle Stick Picture Frame

27. Plastic Lid Drip Shield

**#28**   **KNOW WHERE YOUR FOOD COMES FROM.**

Food comes from the Earth! Specific foods are grown in certain climates or different seasons. Many of our favorite foods come from plants, and knowing which plants feed us can help us appreciate them. The more we learn, the more we care for the people, animals, and land where the plants are grown. Can you match these food items with the plants they're made from?

French fries

bread

corn

pizza sauce

tortilla chips

potato

tomato

wheat

Answers: French fries = potatoes; pizza sauce = tomatoes; bread = wheat; tortilla chips = corn.

## #29 VISIT A FARM STAND OR FARMER'S MARKET.

The food sold at most farm stands and farmer's markets is grown or produced locally. Eating food that was grown close to where you live helps reduce pollution from trucks, boats, and planes that would otherwise carry the food from far away. At markets like these, you'll also learn which foods grow in which seasons. Eating seasonally means foods are fresh and we use little or no energy to store them.

If you see something you don't recognize, ask! Trying new foods is fun. Taste-testing leads us to find new favorites. When we learn to like more foods, we become less picky and can eat more sustainably—which means we do less harm to the Earth.

## #30 BRING YOUR OWN UTENSILS AND CONTAINERS.

When eating out, avoid using plastic forks and spoons that will be thrown in the garbage. Bring containers with you for takeout or leftovers. Remember, plastic doesn't decompose and causes harm to animals and plants.

## #31 CARRY A REUSABLE WATER BOTTLE.

Using a reusable bottle is one of the best ways you can reduce pollution. Give yourself bonus points if you have a long-lasting metal or glass bottle that you use many, many times over the course of several years.

## #32 EAT YOUR FRUITS AND VEGGIES!

Why? There are lots of reasons! First, all fruits and nearly all vegetables grow on plants that flower—which pollinators, like bees, need to survive. Next, plants have leaves, which help to clean the air we breathe. Vegetables and fruits can also often be purchased without any packaging. Plants are foods we can compost to help enrich the soil and grow new plants! (More on composting on page 54.) Plus, fruits and veggies are good for you and give you long-lasting energy to complete more green activities!

## #33 SAVE SOME FOR LATER.

Put leftovers in a tight container and mark it with your name. Save energy by cooking once and eating the same thing for two or more meals.

**DID YOU KNOW?**
Studies show that an average person uses more than 150 plastic water bottles in a year. Your reusable bottle makes a BIG difference!

# CHAPTER 3

# TECHnically Speaking!

## Earth-Friendly Fun and Games

Can we make a screen "green"? Why, yes, in fact, we may. With some tips, we can use less energy today!

**#34** **USE AIRPLANE MODE.**
Putting a phone or tablet on Airplane Mode saves battery life. (And you don't have to be on a plane to use it!) The longer your battery lives, the less you'll have to charge it, and the less energy you'll use overall.

## #35 SHUT IT DOWN.

A screen that's in Sleep Mode is still using energy! Shut down/power off computers and video games when you're not using them.

## #36 UNPLUG.

With a grown-up's permission, unplug or turn off a power strip. Small amounts of electric current—called phantom or vampire loads—can run from a wall outlet through an electrical cord even when a device is turned off. Save energy by unplugging electronics (TV, computer, video games) or switching off the power strip when you're away at school or on a trip.

## CHOOSE THE RIGHT BATTERY.

Use rechargeable (multi-use) batteries for highly used electronics such as cameras, flashlights, and toys. If you have items that you don't use often, single-use batteries have the least impact on the environment. Remember: never throw any kind of battery in the trash—batteries contain harmful substances! Check Call2Recycle.org or Earth911.com to find out where you can recycle dead batteries.

## #38 TAKE CARE OF YOUR THINGS. 🗑 ♻

Pick up your toys and use electronics gently. You reduce waste when your stuff lasts longer and doesn't become useless or have to be replaced. Instead of throwing away toys you've outgrown, donate or sell them so they can be used by someone else.

Donations

## #39 THINK CREATIVELY. 🗑

If a game is missing a part, can you make a substitute piece?

# #40 GET (OR USE) A LIBRARY CARD!

A library card allows you to borrow instead of buying things brand new. Many libraries have movies, music, games, books, ebooks, magazines, and even Wi-Fi devices. Saving the planet is fun—and free!

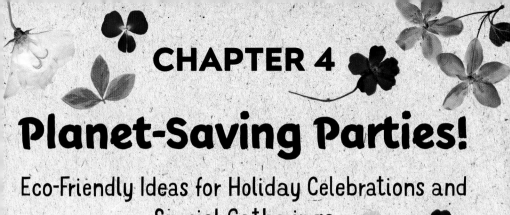

# CHAPTER 4

# Planet-Saving Parties!

## Eco-Friendly Ideas for Holiday Celebrations and Special Gatherings

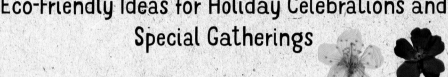

**#41 – #43 D-ECO-RATE!**

Choose natural or recyclable decorations, which keep excess plastic out of landfills.

**41. Recycled-Paper or Dried-Flower Confetti**

**42. Paper Bag Placemats and/or Tablecloths That Guests Can Write On!**

**43. Wildflower Centerpiece**

## #44 TRY ALTERNATIVES TO WRAPPING PAPER.

Use newspapers, magazines, or grocery store bags to wrap gifts. You can even decorate the outside with your own artwork! Or place the present in a basket or bowl and wrap it with reused or reusable cloth.

### #45 MAKE ECO-GLITTER!

Decorate a card with homemade sparkles. If they spill, no big deal—eco-glitter is made from natural or biodegradable materials. (You may want to wipe them up so ants don't come around, though!)

sugar (use brown, white, or dyed sugar for colorful effects)

pink or white salt

crushed candy

store-bought cellulose glitter

### #46 GIVE NATURAL PARTY FAVORS.

Want to give everyone a gift bag? Try filling paper or cloth bags with eco-friendly creations instead of plastic toys. Ideas include sidewalk chalk, home-baked goods, homemade play dough, birdseed balls, seed- or wood-bead bracelets, or pine-cone ornaments. Use a search engine to find instructions for all these crafts.

# #47 – #52 PLAY GAMES THAT DON'T USE ELECTRICITY OR DISPOSABLE PLASTIC.

47. Hide-and-Seek

48. Hand-Clapping Games

49. Tag

50. Beanbag Toss

51. Obstacle Course

52. Sports

# CHAPTER 5

# The Great Outdoors!

## Fresh Ideas for Helping the Earth Around You

**#53** **MAKE A WISH!** 🌱 🌳
Have you every blown on a puffy
dandelion and made a wish? Not only
is this fun to do, but you're actually
spreading seeds! Dandelions bloom earlier
in the spring than most flowers, making them
a good food source for hungry bees.

## #54 BE YOUR OWN MOTOR.

Moving around using a bike, scooter, skateboard, or roller skates saves fuel and is great for the environment. The only energy required comes from YOU!

## #55 MAKE A READING FORT.

Find a space where you can read environmental books and take notice of the wildlife around you. A park, playground, or even a spot indoors near a window will do. To make a fort, try using an old sheet tied to a tree branch or tucked into a dresser drawer. It will give you privacy indoors, and act as a sun shade outdoors. Suggestions for what to read are listed at the end of this book!

**#56**

## PLANT A TREE!

Arbor Day—the last Friday in April—is a holiday when people are encouraged to plant trees. Not only do trees help make the world more beautiful, but their leaves absorb carbon dioxide—a gas that can be harmful to breathe. Their leaves also produce oxygen—a gas we need to breathe to stay alive. For tips on choosing, planting, and growing trees, see pages 82–83.

**DID YOU KNOW?**
One average hardwood tree can absorb 48 pounds of carbon dioxide every year. That's kind of like each tree drinking six gallons of pollution per year to help us clean up the air!

## #57 LEARN TO TRANSPLANT.

Remember those onions or potatoes you planted in containers? You can start an outdoor garden if you or your school has a sunny space outdoors by transplanting whatever plants or seeds you've started growing inside.

> To **transplant** means to safely dig up and replant a plant in a new area or a different container. There are lots of online videos that can teach you how!

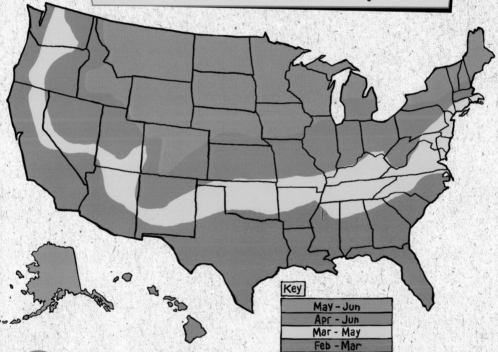

| Key |
|---|
| May – Jun |
| Apr – Jun |
| Mar – May |
| Feb – Mar |

## #58 KNOW YOUR GROWING ZONE. 

Understanding your local climate is important if you want to help it. Can you find your growing zone? Tap your finger on the spot where you live. Take note of the color of your zone. Then, drag your finger to the key to figure out when you should plant (or transplant) your garden outside.

# #59

## COMPOST!

Play with your food!
Get your hands dirty! You can reduce
the amount of food waste thrown in the garbage
by *composting*—letting food scraps and yard waste
break down and turn into usable dirt.

Composting is fun to do and makes a great family
or community project, but it does require planning.
You'll need the right outdoor space, some hard work,
and a commitment in order to maintain your pile. Still
interested? You can find out more by visiting the
Rodale Institute (rodaleinstitute.org/blog/backyard
-composting-basics-a-cheatsheet/) or the U.S.
Environmental Protection Agency (epa.gov/recycle
/composting-home).

## #60 TURN OFF THE HOSE! 💧

When you're not using the hose, make sure it's shut completely off. If it's dripping or leaking, tell a grown-up right away. Water plants in the morning and evening, when it's cooler. That way more water will seep into the soil and less will dry up in the heat of the sun.

**DID YOU KNOW?**
According to the EPA, "A leaky faucet that drips at the rate of one drip per second can waste more than 3,000 gallons per year." That's enough to fill the barrel of a concrete mixer truck!

## #61 COLLECT RAINWATER. 🪣

Although you shouldn't drink it, your plants can! Put your watering can outside to collect water when it rains. This prevents you from having to fill it with water from a faucet. Remember to use the water within one day of the rain to avoid it becoming a mosquito nursery. (Mosquitoes lay their eggs in shallow puddles and the wet walls of containers!)

## #62 LOVE BUGS!

Some people swat at insects or spray them with poison. But many insects are good for plants, animals, and people. Learning more about these creatures allows us to appreciate how important they are, and how we can welcome them in the outdoor spaces near our homes.

I spread pollen from flower to flower so crops can grow—and I make delicious honey!

I tunnel through soil, letting air and water get to the roots of plants. And I'm NOT an insect!

I help plants by eating bugs that harm them, like aphids.

I take care of pesky flies and even the occasional mosquito. (You're welcome! And I'm not an insect, either.)

I'm a hunter with great eyesight. I'm fun to watch, and I eat lots of pesky insects.

# Make a bee hotel.

Many bees travel alone and need safe places to rest. Here's how to make them a place to stay—from recycled materials!

## You'll need:

- 12 sheets of printer or construction paper (reused or upcycled is best!)
- 2 sheets of paper towel or recycled newspaper
- 2 rubber bands
- tape
- an empty juice carton, quart-sized (washed and dried)

Roll the paper into long, skinny tubes about the width of a coin. Tape each one to keep it from unrolling, and divide the tubes into two bunches. Use a rubber band to gently secure each bunch, then wrap each bunch in a paper towel or sheet of newspaper. With an adult's help, cut the top off the juice carton and slide the bundle of tubes inside. Place your bee hotel on its side in a shady spot that won't get wet, close to flowering plants. You're ready to welcome guests!

## #63 BECOME A COMMUNITY SCIENTIST.

Scientists do research and collect information—called data—that helps us understand our world. But guess what? Kids can do research and contribute to scientists' efforts, too! When non-scientists team up to help with scientific research, we call it community science. Two groups of animals that many community-scientists (including kids) can easily help are butterflies and birds.

Community Science Butterfly Activity: Track Monarch Butterflies! Learn how to spot a monarch egg, caterpillar, or butterfly. Then log online and report your sighting at JourneyNorth.org or MonarchWatch.org.

Community Science Bird Activity: Backyard Bird Count! Identify the birds you see in your backyard or a nearby park and make a report to GBBC.Birdcount.org. Many people around the world do this on special days in February each year.

In many places, bird and butterfly populations have been declining. Extend your community science activities by encouraging native birds and butterflies to live in your area, with special gardens or houses.

A pollinator garden attracts butterflies. Research which butterflies live in your area and plant what they like to eat or lay their eggs on. (For example, monarchs like milkweed, swallowtails like dill and fennel, and endangered Karner blues like wild lupine.) If you don't have a yard, you can plant in containers to set outside on a fire escape or stoop. Don't forget that butterflies also need water. You can make a bath for them by placing marbles or rocks and water in a shallow pan.

As humans build homes and buildings, we often mow plants that birds and pollinators love, such as clover and dandelions. We also cut down trees where birds once made their homes. Providing a birdhouse gives bird families a safe place to nest in areas that birds and humans share. If you aren't able to build or buy a wooden birdhouse, you can easily make one from a recycled juice carton.

## #66 "BIRD-PROOF" YOUR WINDOWS! 🤍

Many birds migrate from one place to another during the winter to find food and locations to nest. It can be a dangerous trip. Along the way, a lot of birds injure themselves by flying into glass windows. Help make their journey safer by using window clings or hanging suncatchers in your windows to make them more visible. You can even make your own clings with upcycled materials!

## #67 TRACK THAT CAT! 🤍

If you have a cat, be a hero by keeping it indoors where it can't hunt birds. (Outdoor cats kill more than a billion birds each year in the U.S.!)

### #68 FEED THE BIRDS.

Some birds migrate to find food during the winter, but others stay in the same place all year. Here are some ways to feed them in different seasons!

# WINTER

Make a recycled toilet-paper roll birdseed feeder by spreading peanut butter on the cardboard tube, then rolling it on a plate of seeds. Hang your masterpiece in a visible outdoor spot and watch the birds enjoy!

# SPRING

Whenever you're eating an orange, share! Place wedges in highly visible outdoor spots where birds tend to visit. After a day or two, make sure to discard the leftovers. Many birds love dried fruit, too, which will last a little longer than fresh fruit, and you can also place it outside.

# SUMMER

Encourage nectar drinkers, such as orioles and hummingbirds, to visit by making a sugar-water feeder out of a shallow, recycled plastic container with a red lid. With an adult's help, punch four to six sesame-seed-sized holes in the lid. Mix 1 cup water with 1/4 cup sugar, and pour it into the container. (Make more mix if your container is larger.) Put the lid back on the container and place it outside on a fence or table, or hang it from a tree branch. Birds can fit their beaks into the holes to drink. Yum!

You'll want to clean the feeder, change the sugar-water mix, and check for ants every day.

# FALL

With an adult's help, cut the top off a small pumpkin and hollow it out, removing the seeds. Then pierce the sides of the pumpkin with a couple of sticks to create places for birds to sit. Fill the pumpkin with birdseed and place it on a table, or hang it from a tree using rope. Birds will get a tasty snack as they prepare for winter or a long migration.

### #69 OBEY THE RULES.

At parks and beaches, read all signs. The rules on them—such as staying on the trails, not feeding wildlife, and leaving no trace—help animals, plants, and people. Following guidelines set in place by experts is one of the best ways we can keep our Earth beautiful and natural.

### #70 HAVE A CHIT-CHAT.

Yes—talking really *can* help the Earth! When you're at a park or museum, ask questions and talk to the staff or guides. The more you know, the more you can help. Don't forget to share what you learn with friends and family!

### #71 KEEP A BAG HANDY.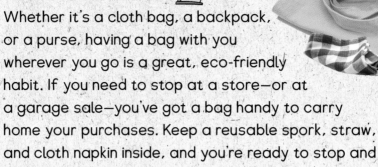

Whether it's a cloth bag, a backpack, or a purse, having a bag with you wherever you go is a great, eco-friendly habit. If you need to stop at a store—or at a garage sale—you've got a bag handy to carry home your purchases. Keep a reusable spork, straw, and cloth napkin inside, and you're ready to stop and eat, too!

### #72 SEE, THEN DO.

If you see litter—and it looks safe to pick up—go for it! By putting litter where it belongs (in the garbage), you help keep it out of our lakes, rivers, and oceans, where it can harm animals. Be sure to wash your hands or use sanitizer afterward.

### #73 SCOOP SAFELY.

Grossed out by garbage? Avoid touching the stuff by cutting a clean milk jug to make a litter scooper. This "hand-y" tool will keep your hands clean!

**#74**

## SHARPEN YOUR NIGHT VISION.

From insects to birds to sea turtles to corals, many animals are negatively affected by artificial light. Daylight and the dark of night are signals for many animals to hunt, eat, sleep, reproduce, or migrate. Changes to the natural rhythm of light days and dark nights can confuse or endanger them. Let's help them by turning off outdoor lights to reduce light pollution.

# CHAPTER 6

# Dress Your Best!

## Eco-Friendly Clothing and Accessory Ideas

### #75 CHECK THE WEATHER.

When you dress for the weather by wearing protective outerwear in rain or snow, your clothes underneath don't get wet and dirty. That way, you won't have to wear (and wash!) extra clothes. When it's hot outside, wear a hat and sunglasses to help you safely stay outside and play longer—outdoor games usually use less energy than indoor electronics.

### #76 STAY WARM.

Wear socks and a sweater around the house on cold days. When you stay warm, you can help your family turn down the heat in your house. This reduces energy and pollution, because a cooler house requires less fossil fuel to burn for heat.

### #77 CLOSE THAT WINDOW!

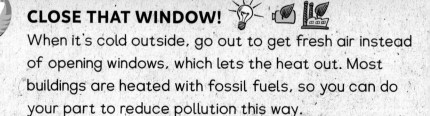

When it's cold outside, go out to get fresh air instead of opening windows, which lets the heat out. Most buildings are heated with fossil fuels, so you can do your part to reduce pollution this way.

## #78 LEARN TO SEW.

Sewing ripped clothes rather than throwing them away or buying new ones reduces our impact on the environment.

If you don't have a needle, or are too young to use one, you can use a round toothpick to practice!

## #79 USE NATURAL DYES. 

With a grown-up's permission, give new life to an old pillowcase or T-shirt by tie-dyeing it with foods from around the house (beets, coffee, turmeric, blueberries, blackberries). Natural dyes are biodegradable and don't have chemicals in them that might be harmful to our water or soil.

### #80 HOST A CLOTHING SWAP. 🗑️ ♻️

Invite friends over and ask everyone to bring clothes they've outgrown or no longer want. Donate leftovers to charity—or organize a garage sale to earn some spending money!

### #81 MAKE NATURAL OR RECYCLED JEWELRY. 🗑️ 💙

A lot of jewelry is made of plastic that doesn't decompose. Try making bracelets out of recycled material, such as by braiding plastic bags, to keep them out of landfills. Or use natural materials such as seeds or wooden beads to string necklaces on cotton or silk thread. A piece of jewelry made of natural items will biodegrade if it's discarded.

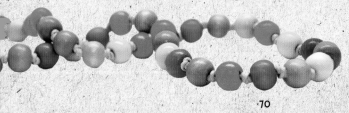

# #82 WEAR A RECYCLED COSTUME.

When it's time to dress up for a play or holiday, think outside the (upcycled) box! Borrow a costume from a friend or make your own. Here are some upcycle ideas.

recycled-box robot

pizza delivery person

ballerina with reused-paper tutu

recycle bin costume

# CHAPTER 7

# Student Power!

## Earth-Friendly Classroom Ideas

**#83** **LET THE LIGHT SHINE IN.**
Ask your teacher to turn out the lights on sunny days if your classroom has windows.

**#84** **USE BOTH SIDES.**
In your notebook or on your homework, use the front and back of each page without skipping pages, if you can.

**DID YOU KNOW?**
Paper is one of the easiest items for people to recycle. Many recycling machines even remove the staples from paper, so don't worry about taking them out.

**#85**

## BE INSPIRED.

Write a story or song, or do an art project that celebrates Earth. Use natural items like chalk, sticks, rocks, or paper scraps to tell your stories or make your art.

> **DID YOU KNOW?**
> Most paper is made from trees.

**#86**

## JOIN YOUR SCHOOL'S ENVIRONMENTAL CLUB.

If you don't have one, ask if you can start one! Your group can meet and share ideas and resources, and even work together, to help accomplish the tasks in this book and beyond! Student projects across the world help the Earth in many ways, from planting gardens to making communities aware of environmental problems and solutions. With your teachers, classmates, and community helping out, you have even more power to make change.

**#87**

**START A RECYCLED-INSTRUMENT BAND.**

Suggest this activity to your music teacher or start a fun recess or after-school activity! Upcycle items commonly found around the school, such as buckets, plastic containers, or cardboard boxes that will make noises when tapped or shaken. Collect broken pencils and crayons to use as fillers. Your instruments and any lyrics you write for songs can spread the message of the Lorax!

We've got buckets for drums,
containers full of crumbs.
We shake and rattle. The Lorax sings.
Meet our band, the Eco-Things!

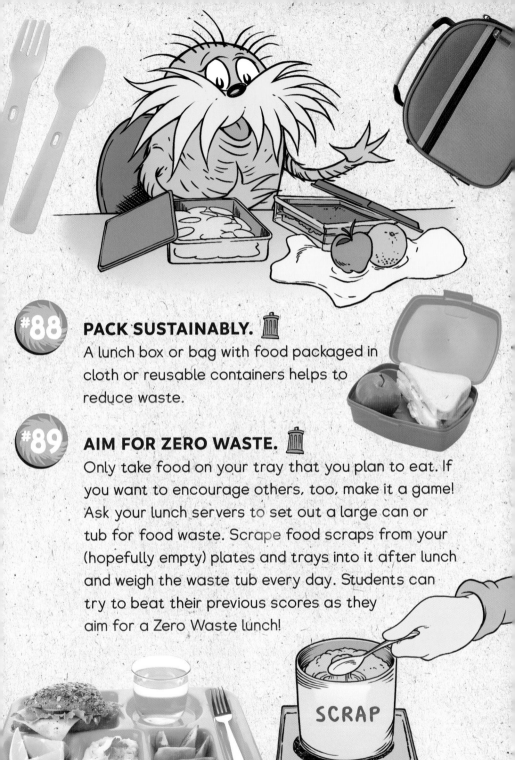

### #88 PACK SUSTAINABLY. 🗑

A lunch box or bag with food packaged in cloth or reusable containers helps to reduce waste.

### #89 AIM FOR ZERO WASTE. 🗑

Only take food on your tray that you plan to eat. If you want to encourage others, too, make it a game! Ask your lunch servers to set out a large can or tub for food waste. Scrape food scraps from your (hopefully empty) plates and trays into it after lunch and weigh the waste tub every day. Students can try to beat their previous scores as they aim for a Zero Waste lunch!

## #90 ORGANIZE!

With your teacher's help, organize a school field trip to a nature center, state park, or other environmental location. Many local businesses and organizations are happy to host or sponsor class trips or events. Ask your teacher to find out how to make arrangements. Field trip suggestions, anyone?

NATIONAL PARK SERVICE

Department of the Interior

## SWAP ROLES! BE A TEACHER!

Have you been doing things at home to help the Earth?
Do a presentation in school for show-and-tell and share
what you've been up to. Inspire others to go green!

**GREEN YOUR FUTURE!**

No, it's not time to get a job! But there are many green careers you can learn about now, to help shape your thinking as you grow up. Here are just a few.

# WHO'S THAT WORKER?

Can you match the job title with the description of what that person does?

**1. Beekeeper**

**2. Sanitation Worker**

**3. Organic Farmer**

**4. National Park Guide**

**5. Veterinarian**

**6. Science Teacher**

a. instructs students about the physical and natural world

b. operates trash and recycling trucks to help keep streets and cities clean

c. grows crops or raises animals (e.g., cows, chickens) without using synthetic (human-made) chemicals

d. treats sick or injured animals in clinics, zoos, or the wild

e. takes care of bees that pollinate crops and/or make honey

f. helps visitors follow rules and shares information about animals, plants, and protected lands

## #93 TURN IN HOMEWORK ONLINE.

Ask your teacher if you can turn in homework
through the computer without printing it at all.
No paper or ink needed!

## #94 SHUT DOWN LEARNING DEVICES AND ELECTRONICS.

Turn off your school and home computers, tablets,
TVs, or personal devices when you are not using them
overnight. Put them in sleep mode when you are not
using them during the day.

**#95**

**SAVE SUPPLIES.**
At the end of the year, box up any leftover supplies and reuse them the following year.

SHUT DOWN

**ECO-JOKE:**

What did the pencil say to the kid who reused school supplies?

You're even sharper than I am!

## #96 PLANT A CLASS TREE. 🌳 💚 🏭

If you have room on your school grounds, ask your teacher if you and your classmates can plant a tree. Break into three teams to decide the following:

**What kind of tree?** Research native species—these are trees that grow naturally in your area. You want a tree that will be resistant to disease, lives long, does not require a lot of maintenance, and grows to be the size you want. A local environmental center, university, or botanist can help you choose and find a sapling.

**Where should it go?** Trees need sunshine, good soil, room underground for their roots to spread, and overhead clearance so they won't grow into power lines, for example.

**How will you care for it?** The third group can make sure that the tree is planted correctly and kept healthy. This team might make a plan for protecting the tree from wildlife, wind damage, or harmful insects. They can also make a plaque with information about the tree so others learn about it and respect it for years to come.

**DID YOU KNOW?**
If you plant an oak tree in first grade, it could be twenty feet tall or higher by the time you graduate high school!

# CHAPTER 8

# Green Your World!

## Environmentalism in Your Community

**#97** **CELEBRATE!**

Many days on the calendar are set aside for holidays and festivals featuring activities that encourage us to "green" our planet. These days would be great opportunities to try some of the tasks in this book!

**February 2:** World Wetlands Day (global)

**March 22:** World Water Day (global)

**April 22:** Earth Day (global)

**Last Friday in April\*** Arbor Day (U.S.)

**Third Friday in May:** Endangered Species Day (U.S.)

**May 22:** International Day for Biological Diversity (global)

**June 5:** World Environment Day (global)

**July 29:** International Tiger Day (global)

**September 22:** World Car-Free Day (global)

**October 4:** World Animal Day (global)

\*You can check here to see if your state observes Arbor Day on a day that is best for planting trees in your area (arborday.org/celebrate/dates.cfm).

### #98 VISIT A RECYCLING CENTER OR LOCAL COMPOSTING SITE. 🗑️ ♻️

Yes, even whole cities compost! When you visit, you'll discover helpful tips to use in your home or community.

### #99 RAISE FUNDS. 🤍

Host a lemonade stand or yard sale to earn money for an organization that helps the environment. You could also use the funds to participate in an adopt-an-endangered-animal program. Adoption programs like this don't deliver animals to your door, but they *do* help keep animals safe in their own wild habitats. Sometimes, you'll get an update with pictures on how your animal is doing. Learn more about these programs through the World Wildlife Fund (worldwildlife.org).

## #100 MAKE IT A FAMILY AFFAIR!

Ask your parents if there is an environmental organization you can join as a family. Many environmental groups invite young people to join as members or participate in activities. For a list of suggested organizations, see pages 91–93.

And that brings us to the grand finale. The 101st thing you can do to help the Earth is . . .

### #101 DO NOTHING!

That's right. Sleep in, look at the sky, stare out the window. When we do less, our brain is often able to do *more!* And we need our brains in good shape to help the Earth. So, every once in a while, take a break. Relax. Getting some rest is the easiest activity there is, but it's also important. Take care of yourself. By staying positive and refreshed, you can keep helping Planet Earth!

What's that you say?
You say that you care?
You think that it's fun
helping forests and air?

Each deed that we do
has its very own worth.
If we keep up the ⌃FUN work,
we can save Planet Earth!

# For Further Reading

Let's go read *The Lorax!*
Let's learn science and math!
We can read on the couch.
We can read in the bath!

## Be A Tree!
by Maria Gianferrari, illustrated by Felicita Sala
(Abrams Books for Young Readers).

This poetic book takes a look at the beauty of trees and the wise lessons people can learn from them. For preschoolers and up.

## Compost Stew: An A to Z Recipe for the Earth
by Mary McKenna Siddals, illustrated by Ashley Wolff (Tricycle Press).

This rhymed picture book explains how to start a compost pile and what's safe to include. For preschoolers and up.

## Counting Birds: The Idea That Helped Save Our Feathered Friends
by Heidi E. Y. Stemple, illustrated by Clover Robin (Seagrass Press).

An award-winning picture book that tells the story of ornithologist Frank Chapman, who organized the first annual bird count. For preschoolers and up.

## Earth! My First 4.54 Billion Years
by Stacy McAnulty, illustrated by David Litchfield (Henry Holt and Co.).

This funny illustrated picture book (narrated by Earth herself!) is guaranteed to make you chuckle as you learn about the planet we call home. For preschoolers and up.

## Farmer Will Allen and the Growing Table

by Jacqueline Briggs Martin, illustrated by Eric-Shabazz Larkin,
afterword by Will Allen (Readers to Eaters).

The inspiring true story of African American innovator,
educator, and community builder Will Allen. For kindergarten
and up.

## How to Help the Earth—by the LORAX

with Tish Rabe, illustrated by Christopher Moroney and Jan Gerardi
(Random House, Step into Reading: A Science Reader, Step 3).

A rhymed easy reader in which the Lorax shows simple ways
to help the Earth. For kindergarten and up.

## Me . . . Jane

by Patrick McDonnell (Little, Brown Books for Young Readers).

The Caldecott Honor-winning story of young Jane Goodall,
who would grow up to help animals and the environment.
For grades 1 and up.

## One Little Lot: The 1-2-3s of an Urban Garden

by Diane C. Mullen, illustrated by Oriol Vidal (Charlesbridge).

Readers will count ten ways that a neighborhood comes
together to clean up an unused lot on a city street and turn it
into a vegetable garden. For preschoolers and up.

## One Plastic Bag: Isatou Ceesay and the Recycling Women of the Gambia

by Miranda Paul, illustrated by Elizabeth Zunon (Millbrook Press).

The true story of Isatou Ceesay and the women who
began their country's first plastic recycling cooperative.
For kindergarten and up.

### Rachel Carson and Her Book That Changed the World

by Laurie Lawlor, illustrated by Laura Beingessner
(Holiday House Books for Young Readers).

An award-winning biography of scientist and environmentalist Rachel Carson. For grades 1 and up.

### Seeds of Change: Planting a Path to Peace

by Jen Cullerton Johnson, illustrated by Sonia Lynn Sadler (Lee & Low Books).

Tells the story of Wangari Maathai, the first African woman and environmentalist to win a Nobel Peace Prize.
For grades 2 and up.

### Trash Revolution: Breaking the Waste Cycle

by Erica Fyvie, illustrated by Bill Slavin (Kids Can Press).

A look at the everyday decisions kids make about trash, recycling, and using stuff. For grades 3 and up.

### What a Waste: Trash, Recycling, and Protecting Our Planet

by Jess French (DK Children).

This easy-to-read book tackles all the different ways our actions affect the planet—and how small changes can make a big difference. For grades 1 and up.

# Additional Resources

## Arbor Day Foundation (arborday.org)

The Arbor Day Foundation inspires people to plant, take care of, and celebrate trees. Check out the Carly's Kids Corner section of the site (arborday.org/kids/) to discover games and activities all about trees and why trees are important.

## Audubon Society (audubon.org)

The National Audubon Society protects birds and their habitats. In the Audubon for Kids! section (audubon.org /get-outside/activities/audubon-for-kids), you'll find bird drawings and simple activities you can do at home, in a park, or on a computer.

## Earth Day Network (earthday.org)

The Earth Day Network is growing the world's largest movement for environmental action. On their Take Action page (earthday.org/take-action-now/), visitors can see a total count of reported green acts, take a pledge, or submit their own green idea.

## Jane Goodall Institute (janegoodall.org)

The Jane Goodall Institute was originally created to protect apes and their habitats. Today, the organization also spreads the environmental messages of its founder, Jane Goodall. One of their programs, Roots & Shoots (see janegoodall.org /our-work/our-approach/roots-shoots/), helps young people realize their own strengths and talents so they can quickly find and join matching efforts in their own communities.

## Keep America Beautiful® (kab.org)

Keep America Beautiful is trying to make towns and cities in the United States clean and green. Learn more at their site about how you can participate in national events such as the TrashDash™, America Recycles Day®, and the Great American Cleanup®.

## Rodale Institute™ (rodaleinstitute.org)

The Rodale Institute promotes organic farming through research and education. Check out the My First Garden section at the School Gardening Curriculum page (rodaleinstitute.org/education/school-gardening -curriculum/) for tips on growing vegetables and more.

## United Nations Environment Programme (unenvironment.org)

The UNEP assists countries as they work toward sustaining the Earth for future generations. In the Education and Environment section of their website (unenvironment .org/explore-topics/education-environment), you'll find information about initiatives like Earth School (that connects students working from home with the natural world), and you can visit wildfor.life/the-campaign to learn about the Wild for Life campaign, which the UNEP and other organizations have founded. You can even take a virtual safari on the African savanna and visit other ecosystems (wildfor.life /journeys)!